LABOR LAW
Essential Legal Terms Explained You Need To Know About Law On Labor!

DR. PETER JOHNSON

Copyright © 2019

All rights reserved.

ISBN: 9781798804131

TEXT COPYRIGHT © [DR. PETER JOHNSON]

all rights reserved. No part of this guide may be reproduced in any form without permission in writing from the publisher except in the case of brief quotations embodied in critical articles or reviews.

Legal & disclaimer

The information contained in this book and its contents is not designed to replace or take the place of any form of medical or professional advice; and is not meant to replace the need for independent medical, financial, legal or other professional advice or services, as may be required. The content and information in this book have been provided for educational and entertainment purposes only.

The content and information contained in this book have been compiled from sources deemed reliable, and it is accurate to the best of the author's knowledge, information, and belief. However, the author cannot guarantee its accuracy and validity and cannot be held liable for any errors and/or omissions. Further, changes are periodically made to this book as and when needed. Where appropriate and/or necessary, you must consult a professional (including but not limited to your doctor, attorney, financial advisor or such other professional advisor) before using any of the suggested remedies, techniques, or information in this book.

Upon using the contents and information contained in this book, you agree to hold harmless the author from and against any damages, costs, and expenses, including any legal fees potentially resulting from the application of any of the information provided by this book. This disclaimer applies to any loss, damages or injury caused by the use and application, whether directly or indirectly, of any advice or information presented, whether for breach of contract, tort, negligence, personal injury, criminal intent, or under any other cause of action.

You agree to accept all risks of using the information presented inside this book.

You agree that by continuing to read this book, where appropriate and/or necessary, you shall consult a professional (including but not limited to your doctor, attorney, or financial advisor or such other advisor as needed) before using any of the suggested remedies, techniques, or information in this book.

Table of Contents

Introduction 9

General Provisions 10

Interpretation Of Terms 11

State Policies On Labor 12

Rights And Obligations Of Employees 13

Rights And Obligations Of Employers 14

Industrial Relations 15

Prohibited Acts 16

Employment And Creation Of Employment 17

The Right Of Employees To Work 18

The Right Of Employers To Recruit Labor 19

Employment Service Institutions 20

Labor Contract 21

Forms Of Labor Contract 22

Principles Of Entry Into A Labor Contract 23

Obligation To Enter Into A Labor Contract 24

Obligation To Provide Information Before Entering Into A Labor Contract 25

Prohibited Acts Of Employers When Entering Into And Performing Labor Contracts 26

Entry Into Labor Contracts With More Than One Employer..27

Types Of Labor Contract..28

Contents Of A Labor Contract 29

Annexes To A Labor Contract 30

Effectiveness Of A Labor Contract..................................31

Probation 32

Probation Period 33

Wage During The Probation Period................................34

Expiry Of The Probation Period......................................35

Performance Of Jobs Under A Labor Contract................36

Cases Of Suspension Of A Labor Contract......................37

Part-Time Employees 38

Modification And Supplementation Of A Labor Contract........39

Cases Of Termination Of A Labor Contract....................40

The Right Of Employees To Unilaterally Terminate Labor Contracts..41

The Right Of Employers To Unilaterally Terminate Labor Contracts..42

Cases In Which An Employer Is Prohibited From Unilaterally Terminating A Labor Contract 43

Cancellation Of Unilateral Termination Of A Labor Contract.44

Labor Utilization Plan 45

Severance Allowance 46

Job-Loss Allowance 47

Invalid Labor Contracts 48

Competence To Declare Labor Contract To Be Invalid 49

Labor Lease 50

Labor Leasing Enterprises 51

Labor Leasing Contract 52

Rights And Obligations Of A Labor Leasing Enterprise 53

Rights And Obligations Of The Hiring Party 54

Rights And Obligations Of A Leased Employee 55

Apprenticeship And Vocational Training 56

Responsibilities Of An Employer For Training And Retraining For Vocational Qualification And Skill Improvement 57

Vocational Training Contract Between An Employer And An Employee And Job Training Expenses 58

Wages 59

Minimum Wage 60

Forms Of Wage Payment 61

Wage Payment Period 62

Principles Of Wage Payment 63

Advance Of Wage 64

Deductions From Wages 65

Bonuses 66

Normal Working Time 67

Working Hours At Night 68

Overtime Work 69

Rest Breaks During Working Hours 70

Breaks Between Shifts 71

Weekly Breaks 72

Annual Leave 73

Personal Leave, Unpaid Leave 74

Labor Discipline 75

Internal Working Regulations 76

Principles And Order For Handling Violations Of Labor Discipline 77

Forms Of Handling Of Violations Of Labor Discipline 78

Application Of Dismissal As A Form Of Discipline 79

Prohibited Acts When Handling Violations Of Labor Discipline 80

Work Suspension 81

Compensation For Damage 82

Labor Accidents 83

Occupational Diseases 84

Employers' Responsibilities For Labor Accidents And Occupational Diseases Of Employees 85

Rights Of Employees Who Have Labor Accidents Or Suffer Occupational Diseases 86

Prohibited Acts In Occupational Safety And Hygiene 87

Occupational Safety And Hygiene Plans 88

Personal Protection Equipment In Work 89

Information On Occupational Safety And Hygiene 90

Health Care For Employees 91

State Policies Toward Female Employees 92

Obligations Of Employers Toward Female Employees 93

Protection Of Maternity For Female Employees 94

Right Of Pregnant Employees To Unilaterally Terminate Or Postpone Labor Contracts 95

Maternity Leave 96

Allowances For Leave For Caring A Sick Child, For Pregnancy Checks-Up And For Applying Contraceptive Measures 97

Prohibited Work For Female Employees 98

Minor Employees 99

Employment Of Minors 100

Principles Of Employment Of Minors 101

Prohibited Jobs And Workplaces For Minor Employees 102

Elderly Employees 103

Employment Of Elderly Employees 104

Employment Of Disabled Persons 105

Prohibited Acts In Employment Of Disabled Persons 106

Conclusion 107

Check Out Other Books 108

Introduction

Thank you and congratulate you for downloading the book *"LABOR LAW: Essential Legal Terms Explained You Need To Know About Law On Labor"*

With a clear, concise, and engaging writing style, Dr. Peter Johnson will help you with a practical understanding of labor law topics about *rights and obligations of employees, rights and obligations of employers, labor contract, wage, the right of employees/employers to unilaterally terminate labor contracts, job-loss allowance, invalid labor contracts, apprenticeship and vocational training, normal working time, working hours at night, overtime work, rest breaks during working hours, annual leave, personal leave, unpaid leave, labor discipline, minor employees* and help you build a foundation for understanding the overall picture and much much more. This book delivers extensive coverage of every aspect of the law and details the duties a paralegal is expected to perform when working within law on labor. High-level, comprehensive coverage is combined with cutting-edge developments and foundational concepts.

As the author of the book, I promise this book will be an invaluable source of legal reference for professionals, international lawyers, law students, business professionals and anyone else who want to improve their use of legal terminology, succinct clarification of legal terms and have a better understanding of labor law. All legal terms and phrases are well written and explained clearly in plain English.

Thank you again for purchasing this book, and I hope you enjoy it.

Let's get started!

GENERAL PROVISIONS

The Labor Code regulates labor relations between the salaried employee and the employer, and the other social relations directly related to labor relations.

The Labor applies to all employees as well as all organizations and individuals employing labor according to labor contracts in all economic sectors and of all forms of ownership.

This Labor Code also applies to the apprentices, house workers and a number of other jobs defined in this Code.

INTERPRETATION OF TERMS

1. *Employee* means a person who is full 15 years or older, has the ability to work, works under a labor contract, is paid with wage and is managed and controlled by an employer.

2. *Employer* means an enterprise, an agency, an organization, a cooperative, a household or an individual that hires or employs employees under labor contracts; if the employer is an individual, he/she must have full civil act capacity.

3. *Employees' collective* means an organized group of employees working for the same employer or in the same division within the organizational apparatus of an employer.

4. *Representative organization of a grassroots-level employees' collective* means the executive committee of the grassroots-level trade union or the executive committee of the immediate higher-level trade union in a non-unionized enterprise.

5. *Employers' representative organization* means a lawfully established organization which represents and protects the employers' rights and legitimate interests in industrial relations.

6. *Industrial relation* means a social relation arising from the hiring or employment and wage payment between an employee and an employer.

7. *Labor dispute* means a dispute over rights, obligations or interests which arise between the parties in industrial relations.

Labor dispute comprises individual labor dispute between an employee and an employer, and collective labor dispute between an employees' collective and an employer.

8. *Right-based collective labor dispute* means a dispute between an employees' collective and an employer which arises from different explanations and implementations of the labor law, collective labor agreements, internal working regulations, and other regulations and lawful agreements.

9. *Interest-based collective labor dispute* means a labor dispute arising from the request of an employees' collective for the establishment of new working conditions compared to those stipulated by the labor law, collective labor agreement, internal working regulations, or other regulations and lawful agreements reached in the negotiation process between the employees' collective and the employer.

10. *Forced labor* means the use of force or threat to use force or other tricks to force a person to work against his/her will.

STATE POLICIES ON LABOR

1. To guarantee the rights and legitimate interests of employees; to encourage agreements providing employees with conditions more favorable than those provided by the labor law; and to adopt policies which enable employees to purchase shares and make capital contributions for production and business development.

2. To guarantee the rights and legitimate interests of employers, to ensure lawful, democratic, fair and civilized labor management, and to promote their social responsibility.

3. To create favorable conditions for job creation, self-employment and vocational training and learning in order to acquire employment, and for labor-intensive production and business activities.

4. To adopt policies on the development and distribution of human resources; to provide vocational training, training, retraining and improvement of occupational knowledge and skills for employees, and give preferences for employees with high professional and technical qualifications meeting the requirements of national industrialization and modernization.

5. To adopt policies on labor market development and diversify types of linkage between labor supply and demand.

6. To guide employees and employers to hold dialogues and collective bargains to establish harmonious, stable and progressive industrial relations.

RIGHTS AND OBLIGATIONS OF EMPLOYEES

1. An employee has the following rights:

a/ To work, freely choose a job or occupation, to participate in vocational training and to improve occupational skills and suffer no discrimination;

b/ To receive a wage commensurate with his/her occupational knowledge and skills on the basis of an agreement reached with the employer; to receive labor protection and work in assured conditions of labor safety and labor hygiene; to take leaves according to the prescribed regime, paid annual leaves and enjoy collective welfare benefits;

c/ To form and join and participate in activities of trade unions, occupational associations and other organizations in accordance with law; to request and participate in dialogues with the employer, implement democracy regulations and be consulted at the workplace to protect his/her rights and legitimate interests; and to participate in management activities according to the employer's regulations;

d/ To unilaterally terminate the labor contract in accordance with law;

e/ To go on strike.

2. An employee has the following obligations:

a/ To perform the labor contract and collective labor agreement;

b/ To obey labor discipline and internal working regulations and follow lawful administration of the employer;

c/ To implement the laws on social insurance and health insurance.

RIGHTS AND OBLIGATIONS OF EMPLOYERS

1. An employer has the following rights:

a/ To recruit, arrange and manage employees according to the requirements of production and business; to perform commendation work and handle violations of labor discipline;

b/ To form, join and operate in occupational associations and other organizations in accordance with law;

c/ To request the employees' collective to have dialogue, negotiate and sign a collective labor agreement; to participate in the resolution of labor disputes and strikes; to exchange opinions with the trade union on issues related to industrial relations and improvement of the material and spiritual lives of employees;

d/ To temporarily close the workplace.

2. An employer has the following obligations:

a/ To perform the labor contracts, collective labor agreement and other agreements with employees, to respect the honor and dignity of employees;

b/ To establish a mechanism for and hold dialogue with the employees' collective at the enterprise and strictly implement the regulations on grassroots-level democracy;

c/ To keep a labor management book and a wage book and produce them to competent agencies upon request;

d/ To declare the use of labor within 30 days from the date of commencement of operation, and report periodically on changes in the labor in the process of operation to the local state management agency of labor;

e/ To implement other provisions of law on labor, social insurance and health insurance.

INDUSTRIAL RELATIONS

1. Industrial relations between an individual employee or the employees' collective and an employer must be established through dialogue, negotiation and agreement based on the principles of voluntariness, good faith, equality, cooperation and mutual respect for each other's rights and legitimate interests.

2. Trade unions and the employers' representative organizations shall, in collaboration with state agencies, facilitate the establishment of harmonious, stable and progressive industrial relations; supervise the implementation of the labor law; and protect the rights and legitimate interests of employees and employers.

PROHIBITED ACTS

1. Discriminating on the basis of gender, race, skin color, social strata, marital status, belief, religion, HIV infection, disabilities or for the reason of establishing, joining trade unions and participating in trade union activities.

2. Maltreating employees and committing sexual harassment at the workplace.

3. Forcing labor.

4. Making use of apprenticeship or on-the-job training for the purpose of self-seeking and exploiting labor, or enticing or compelling apprentices or on-the-job trainees to carry out illegal activities.

5. Using employees who have no vocational training or national occupational skills certificates for the occupations or jobs which require employees who have received vocational training or national occupational skills certificates.

6. Enticing, promising or making false advertising to deceive employees or making use of employment services or the sending of labor to work abroad under contracts to commit illegal acts.

7. Illegally using minor employees.

EMPLOYMENT AND CREATION OF EMPLOYMENT

1. Employment is any income-generating laboring activity that is not prohibited by law.

2. The State, employers and the society have the responsibility to create employment and guarantee that all people with working ability have access to employment opportunities.

THE RIGHT OF EMPLOYEES TO WORK

1. To work for any employer in any location that is not prohibited by law.

2. To directly contact an employer or through an employment service institution in order to find a job that meets his/her expectation, capacity, occupational qualification, and health.

THE RIGHT OF EMPLOYERS TO RECRUIT LABOR

An employer has the right to recruit labor directly or through employment service institutions and labor leasing institutions, to increase or reduce the number of employees according to production and business requirements.

EMPLOYMENT SERVICE INSTITUTIONS

1. Employment service institutions have the function of providing job counseling and placement services and vocational training to employees; supplying and recruiting employees at the request of employers; collecting and providing information about the labor market; and performing other tasks in accordance with law.

2. Employment service institutions include employment service centers and employment service enterprises.

Employment service centers are established and operate under the Government's regulations.

Employment service enterprises are established and operate under the Law on Enterprises and must have a license to provide employment services granted by the provincial-level state management agency of labor.

3. Employment service institutions are entitled to collect charges and to tax reduction and exemption in accordance the laws on charges and taxes.

LABOR CONTRACT

Labor contract is an agreement between an employee and an employer on a paid job, working conditions and the rights and obligations of each party in industrial relations.

FORMS OF LABOR CONTRACT

1. A labor contract must be established in writing and made in two copies, one to be kept by the employee and the other by the employer.

2. For temporary jobs with a duration of under 3 months, the parties may enter into a verbal labor contract.

PRINCIPLES OF ENTRY INTO A LABOR CONTRACT

1. Voluntariness, fairness, good faith, cooperation and honesty.

2. Freedom to enter into a labor contract which is not contrary to the law, the collective labor agreement and social morality.

OBLIGATION TO ENTER INTO A LABOR CONTRACT

1. A labor contract must be directly entered into between an employee and an employer before the employee is admitted.

For an employee aged between full 15 years and under 18 years, the labor contract must be entered into with the consent of his/her at-law representative.

2. For a seasonal or specific job that has a duration of under 12 months, a group of employees may authorize a member of the group to enter into a written labor contract; in this case, such labor contract is effective in the same manner as if it is entered into with each of the employees.

A labor contract which is entered into by an authorized person must be enclosed with a list clearly stating the full names, ages, gender, permanent residential addresses, occupations and signatures of all employees concerned.

OBLIGATION TO PROVIDE INFORMATION BEFORE ENTERING INTO A LABOR CONTRACT

1. An employer shall provide an employee with information about the job, workplace, working conditions, working hours, rest time, occupational safety and hygiene, wage, forms of wage payment, social insurance, health insurance, regulations on business confidentiality, technological confidentiality, and other issues directly related to the entry into the labor contract as requested by the employee.

2. The employee shall provide the employer with information about his/her full name, age, gender, residence address, education level, occupational skills and qualification, health conditions and other issues directly related to the entry into a labor contract as requested by the employer.

PROHIBITED ACTS OF EMPLOYERS WHEN ENTERING INTO AND PERFORMING LABOR CONTRACTS

1. Keeping the employees' original identity cards, diplomas and certificates.

2. Requesting employees to make a deposit in cash or property as security for the performance of labor contracts.

ENTRY INTO LABOR CONTRACTS WITH MORE THAN ONE EMPLOYER

An employee may enter into labor contracts with more than one employer, provided that he/she fully performs all the contents of the entered contracts.

In case an employee enters into labor contracts with more than one employer, his/her participation in social insurance and health insurance complies with the Government's regulations.

TYPES OF LABOR CONTRACT

A labor contract must be entered into in one of the following types:

a/ Indefinite-term labor contract;

An indefinite-term labor contract is a contract in which the two parties do not determine the duration and the time of termination of the contract.

b/ Definite-term labor contract;

A definite-term labor contract is a contract in which the two parties determine the duration and the time of termination of the contract within a period of between 12 months and 36 months.

c/ A seasonal or work-specific labor contract that has a duration of under 12 months.

CONTENTS OF A LABOR CONTRACT

A labor contract must have the following principal contents:

a/ Name and address of the employer or the lawful representative of the employer;

b/ Full name, date of birth, gender, residence address, identity card number or other lawful documents of the employee;

c/ Job and workplace;

d/ Term of the labor contract;

e/ Wage, form of wage payment, deadline for wage payment, wage-based allowances and other additional payments;

f/ Regimes for promotion and wage raise;

g/ Working time, rest time;

h/ Labor protection equipment for the employee;

i/ Social insurance and health insurance;

j/ Training, retraining and occupational skill improvement.

ANNEXES TO A LABOR CONTRACT

1. An annex to a labor contract is an integral part of the labor contract and is as valid as the labor contract.

2. An annex to a labor contract details some provisions or amends or supplements the contract.

In case an annex to a labor contract details some provisions that lead to a different understanding of the labor contract, the contents of the labor contract prevail.

In case an annex amends or supplements the labor contract, it must specify the amended or supplemented provisions and the time it takes effect.

EFFECTIVENESS OF A LABOR CONTRACT

A labor contract takes effect on the date it is entered into by the parties, unless otherwise agreed upon by both parties or provided by law.

PROBATION

An employer and an employee may reach agreement on the probation and the rights and obligations of the two parties during the probation period. If reaching agreement on the probation, the two parties may enter into a probation contract.

PROBATION PERIOD

The probation period must be based on the nature and complexity of the job but probation is applied only once for each job and assure the following conditions:

1. It does not exceed 60 days for posts which require professional and technical qualification of collegial or higher level.

2. It does not exceed 30 days for posts which require professional and technical qualifications of intermediate vocational level, professional secondary level, or for technical workers and skilled employees.

3. It does not exceed 6 working days for other types of jobs.

WAGE DURING THE PROBATION PERIOD

The wage for an employee during the probation period must be agreed upon by the two parties but must be at least equal to 85% of the wage for the job.

EXPIRY OF THE PROBATION PERIOD

1. If the probational job is satisfactory, the employer shall sign a labor contract with the employee.

2. During the probation period, each party may cancel the probation agreement without prior notice and compensation if the probational job fails to meet the requirements that have been agreed by the two parties.

PERFORMANCE OF JOBS UNDER A LABOR CONTRACT

The jobs under a labor contract must be performed by the employee who has entered into the contract. The workplace may be as indicated in the labor contract or otherwise agreed upon between the two parties.

CASES OF SUSPENSION OF A LABOR CONTRACT

1. The employee is called up for military service.

2. The employee is held in custody or detention in accordance with the criminal procedure law.

3. The employee is subject to a decision on application of the measure of consignment to a reformatory, compulsory drug detoxification center or compulsory education institution.

4. The female employee is pregnant.

5. Other cases as agreed upon by the two parties.

PART-TIME EMPLOYEES

1. Part-time employee is a person who works for less than the normal daily or weekly working hours as provided by the labor law, the collective labor agreement of the enterprise or the sector or the employer's regulations.

2. An employee may negotiate with the employer on work on a part-time basis when entering into a labor contract.

3. Part-time employees are entitled to a wage and have the same rights and obligations as full-time employees, and are entitled to equal opportunities and to non-discrimination and assured labor safety and hygiene.

MODIFICATION AND SUPPLEMENTATION OF A LABOR CONTRACT

1. During the performance of a labor contract, any party that requests to modify or supplement the contents of the labor contract shall notify at least 3 working days in advance to the other party of the contents to be modified or supplemented.

2. In case the two parties can reach an agreement, the modification or supplementation of the labor contract must be carried out by signing an annex to the labor contract or signing a new labor contract.

3. In case the two parties cannot reach an agreement on the modification or supplementation of the labor contract, they shall continue performing the labor contract already entered into.

CASES OF TERMINATION OF A LABOR CONTRACT

1. The labor contract expires.

2. The work stated in the labor contract has been completed.

3. Both parties agree to terminate the labor contract.

4. The employee fully meets the requirements on the time of payment of social insurance premiums and the age of retirement.

5. The employee is sentenced to imprisonment or death or is prohibited from performing the job stated in the labor contract under a legally effective judgment or ruling of a court.

6. The employee dies or is declared by a court to have lost civil act capacity, be missing or dead.

7. The individual employer dies or is declared by a court to have lost civil act capacity, be missing or dead; the institutional employer terminates operation.

8. The employee is dismissed.

9. The employee unilaterally terminates the labor contract.

10. The employer unilaterally terminates the labor contract; the employer lays off the employee due to structural or technological changes or because of economic reasons, merger, consolidation or division of the enterprise or cooperative.

THE RIGHT OF EMPLOYEES TO UNILATERALLY TERMINATE LABOR CONTRACTS

An employee working under a definite-term labor contract, a seasonal labor contract or performing a certain job of under 12 months may unilaterally terminate the labor contract prior to its expiry in the following cases:

a/ He/she is not assigned to the job or workplace or is not given the working conditions as agreed in the labor contract;

b/ He/she is not paid in full or on time as agreed in the labor contract;

c/ He/she is maltreated, sexually harassed or is subject to forced labor;

d/ He/she is unable to continue performing the labor contract due to personal or family difficulties;

e/ He/she is elected to perform a full-time duty in a people-elected office or is appointed to hold a position in the state apparatus;

f/ A female employee who is pregnant and must take leave as prescribed by a competent health establishment;

g/ If he/she is sick or has an accident and remains unable to work after having received treatment for 90 consecutive days, in case he/she works under a definite-term labor contract, or for a quarter of the contract's term, in case he/she works under a labor contract for a seasonal job or a specific job of under 12 months.

THE RIGHT OF EMPLOYERS TO UNILATERALLY TERMINATE LABOR CONTRACTS

An employer may unilaterally terminate a labor contract in the following cases:

a/ The employee often fails to perform his/her job stated in the labor contract;

b/ The employee is sick or has an accident and remains unable to work after having received treatment for 12 consecutive months, in case he/she works under an indefinite-term labor contract, or for 6 consecutive months, in case he/she works under a definite-term labor contract, or more than half the term of the labor contract, in case he/she works under a labor contract for a seasonal job or a specific job of under 12 months.

When the employee's health has recovered, he/she must be considered for continued entry into the labor contract;

c/ If, as a result of natural disaster, fire or another *force majeure* event as prescribed by law, the employer, though having applied every remedial measure, has to scale down production and cut jobs;

d/ The employee is absent from the workplace after the time limit specified in Article 33 of this Code.

CASES IN WHICH AN EMPLOYER IS PROHIBITED FROM UNILATERALLY TERMINATING A LABOR CONTRACT

1. The employee is sick or has a work accident or occupational disease and is being treated or nursed under the decision of a competent health establishment.

2. The employee is on annual leave, personal leave or any other types of leave permitted by the employer.

3. The employee is on maternity leave in accordance with the Law on Social Insurance.

CANCELLATION OF UNILATERAL TERMINATION OF A LABOR CONTRACT

Each party may cancel its unilateral termination of the labor contract at any time prior to the expiry of the time limit for prior notice by a written notification, provided that such cancellation is agreed by the other party.

LABOR UTILIZATION PLAN

1. A labor utilization plan must have the following principal contents:

a/ The lists and numbers of employees to be further employed and employees to be re-trained for continued employment;

b/ The list and number of employees to be retired;

c/ The lists and numbers of employees to be assigned part-time jobs and those to terminate their labor contracts;

d/ Measures and financial sources for implementing the plan.

2. The labor utilization plan must be elaborated with the participation of the representative organization of the grassroots-level employees' collective.

SEVERANCE ALLOWANCE

1. In case a labor contract terminates, the employer shall pay a severance allowance to the employee who has worked regularly for full 12 months or longer at the rate of half of a month's wage for each working year.

2. The working period used for the calculation of severance allowance is the total period during which the employee actually works for the employer minus the period during which the employee benefits from unemployment insurance in accordance with the Law on Social Insurance, and the working period for which the employee has received severance allowance from the employer.

3. The wage used for the calculation of severance allowance is the average wage in accordance with the labor contract during 6 months preceding the time the employee loses his/her work.

JOB-LOSS ALLOWANCE

1. An employer shall pay a job-loss allowance to an employee who loses his/her job and has worked regularly for the employer for 12 months or longer. The job-loss allowance is equal to 1 month's wage for each working year, but must not be lower than 2 months' wage.

2. The working period used for the calculation of job-loss allowance is the total time during which the employee actually works for the employer minus the time during which the employee benefits from unemployment insurance in accordance with the Law of Social Insurance and the working period for which the employer has paid a severance allowance to the employee.

3. The wage used for the calculation of job-loss allowance is the average wage in accordance with the labor contract during 6 months preceding the time the employee loses his/her job.

INVALID LABOR CONTRACTS

1. A labor contract is wholly invalid in one of the following cases:

a/ The whole contents of the labor contract are illegal;

b/ The labor contract is signed by an incompetent person;

c/ The job agreed upon in the labor contract is prohibited by law;

d/ The contents of the labor contract limit or prevent the employee from exercising the right to establish and join trade unions and participate in trade union activities.

2. A labor contract is partially invalid when one of its contents is illegal but does not affect the remaining contents of the labor contract.

3. In case part or the whole of the labor contract provides the employee's benefits lower than those provided by the labor law, internal labor regulations and collective labor agreement that are currently effective or the contents of the labor contract limit other rights of the employee, such part or the whole of the labor contract is invalid.

COMPETENCE TO DECLARE LABOR CONTRACT TO BE INVALID

1. The labor inspectorates and people's courts are competent to declare labor contracts to be invalid.

2. The Government shall provide the order and procedures for labor inspectorates to declare labor contracts to be invalid.

LABOR LEASE

1. Labor lease means that an enterprise licensed for labor lease recruits an employee to work for another employer and the employee is managed by the hiring employer while still maintaining industrial relations with the leasing enterprise.

2. Labor lease is a conditional business line applicable only to certain jobs.

LABOR LEASING ENTERPRISES

1. A labor leasing enterprise shall pay a deposit and obtain a license for labor lease.

2. The duration of labor lease must not exceed 12 months.

3. The Government shall provide the licensing of labor lease, the payment of deposits and the list of jobs allowed for labor lease.

LABOR LEASING CONTRACT

1. The labor leasing enterprise and the hiring party shall sign a written labor leasing contract, which is made in 2 copies, each to be kept by one party.

2. A labor leasing contract must contain the following principal contents:

a/ Location of the workplace, working position for the leased employee, detailed description of the job and specific requirements for the leased employee;

b/ Duration of the lease; the starting time of the lease;

c/ Working time, rest time, occupational safety and hygiene conditions at the workplace;

d/ Obligations of each party toward the leased employee.

3. The labor leasing contract must not contain any agreement on the rights and benefits of the employee that are less favorable than those agreed upon in the labor contract signed between the employee and the labor leasing enterprise.

RIGHTS AND OBLIGATIONS OF A LABOR LEASING ENTERPRISE

1. To ensure supply of a skilled employee who meets the requirements of the hiring party and the labor contract signed with the employee.

2. To inform the leased employee of the contents of the labor leasing contract.

3. To sign a labor contract with the employee in accordance with the law on labour.

4. To provide the hiring party with a brief personal record of the leased employee and his/her demands.

5. To perform the obligations of an employer in accordance with this Code; to pay wage, wage for public holidays and annual leaves, wage of work suspension, severance allowance, job-loss allowance; compulsory social insurance, health insurance and unemployment insurance premiums for the employee in accordance with law.

To ensure that the wage of the leased employee is not lower than that of a normal employee of the hiring party who has the same qualification and performs the same job or job of equal value.

6. To make a dossier stating the number of leased employees, the hiring party and leasing charges, and report them to the provincial-level state management agency of labor.

7. To discipline leased employees who are returned by the hiring party for their violations of labor discipline.

RIGHTS AND OBLIGATIONS OF THE HIRING PARTY

1. To inform and guide the leased employee to understand its internal working regulations and other regulations.

2. Not to discriminate between the leased employee and its own employees regarding working conditions.

3. To negotiate with the leased employee on working at night or overtime when such working is not included in the labor leasing contract.

4. Not to sub-lease the leased employee.

5. To negotiate with the leased employee and the labor leasing enterprise in order to officially employ this employee in case the labor contract between the leased employee and the labor leasing enterprise have not yet expired.

6. To return to the labor leasing enterprise the leased employee who fails to meet the requirements as agreed or who violates labor discipline.

7. To provide evidence of the leased employee's violation of labor discipline for the labor leasing enterprise to consider and discipline such employee.

RIGHTS AND OBLIGATIONS OF A LEASED EMPLOYEE

1. To perform the job under the labor contract signed with the labor leasing enterprise.

2. To comply with the internal labor regulations, labor discipline, the lawful management and the collective labor agreement of the hiring party.

3. To be paid with a wage not lower than that of employees of the hiring party who have the same qualification and perform the same job or job of equal value.

4. To lodge a complaint with the labor leasing enterprise when the hiring party violates agreements in the labor leasing contract.

5. To exercise the right to unilaterally terminate the labor contract with the labor leasing enterprise.

6. To negotiate to sign a labor contract with the hiring party after terminating the labor contract with the labor leasing enterprise.

APPRENTICESHIP AND VOCATIONAL TRAINING

1. An employee is entitled to choose an occupation and apprenticeship at a workplace which is appropriate to his/her employment demand.

2. The State encourages any eligible employer to establish a vocational training center or open vocational training classes at the workplace in order to train and retrain for improving occupational qualifications and skills for its current employees and providing vocational training for other apprentices in accordance with the law on vocational training.

RESPONSIBILITIES OF AN EMPLOYER FOR TRAINING AND RETRAINING FOR VOCATIONAL QUALIFICATION AND SKILL IMPROVEMENT

1. An employer shall prepare annual training plans and budgets and organize training for improving vocational qualifications and skills for his/her current employees and training for employees before switching them to perform other jobs.

2. An employer shall report on the results of vocational qualification and skill improvement training to the provincial-level state management agency of labor in its annual report on labor.

VOCATIONAL TRAINING CONTRACT BETWEEN AN EMPLOYER AND AN EMPLOYEE AND JOB TRAINING EXPENSES

1. The two parties shall enter into a vocational training contract in case the employee will be trained for vocational qualification and skill improvement or re-trained at home or abroad with the employer's fund, including the fund donated by the employer's partner.

A vocational training contract must be made in 2 copies, each to be kept by one party.

2. A vocational training contract must have the following principal contents:

a/ The trained occupation;

b/ Training venue; training period;

c/ Training expenses;

d/ The period during which the employee commits to working for the employer after training;

e/ Responsibility to reimburse training expenses;

f/ Responsibilities of the employer.

3. Training expenses are those accompanied by valid documents on payment for trainers, training materials, training venues, machinery and equipment, practicing materials, support for learners and wages and social insurance and health insurance premiums paid for learners during the training. In case an employee is sent to a foreign country for training, training expenses also include travel and living expenses during the period of overseas stay.

WAGES

1. Wage is a monetary amount which is paid by an employer to an employee to do a job as agreed by the two parties.

Wage includes a wage amount which is based on the work or title, wage allowance(s) and other additional payments.

An employee's wage must not be lower than the minimum wage set by the Government.

2. A wage must be paid to an employee based on labor productivity and quality of the work performed.

3. An employer shall pay equal wages without gender-based discrimination to employees doing a job of equal value.

MINIMUM WAGE

Minimum wage is the lowest payment for an employee who performs the simplest job in normal working conditions and must ensure the employee's minimum living needs and his/her family.

The minimum wage must be determined on a monthly, daily and hourly basis by region or sector.

FORMS OF WAGE PAYMENT

1. An employer may select the form of wage payment based on working time, products or piecework. The selected form of wage payment must be maintained for a certain period of time. Any change in the form of payment must be informed by the employer to the employee at least 10 days in advance.

2. Wage may be paid by cash or via the employee's personal account opened at a bank. In case the wage is paid into the bank account, the employer shall negotiate with the employee on any fees related to the opening and maintenance of the account.

WAGE PAYMENT PERIOD

1. Employees enjoying hourly, daily or weekly wages must be paid after the working hour, day or week or paid in a lump sum as agreed by the two parties, provided that wages are paid in a lump sum at least every 15 days.

2. Employees enjoying monthly wages must be paid once a month or once every half of the month.

3. Employees enjoying wages based on products or piecework must be paid as agreed by the two parties; if the work is to be performed in a number of months, each month, the employee must be given an advance wage according to the volume of work completed in the month.

PRINCIPLES OF WAGE PAYMENT

An employee must be paid with a full wage in a direct and timely manner.

ADVANCE OF WAGE

1. An employee may be given a wage in advance according to the conditions agreed upon by the two parties.

2. An employer shall advance a wage amount to an employee corresponding to the number of days off which the employee takes to perform citizens' obligations from 1 week to 1 month at most. The employee shall refund this advance amount, except the case that he/she performs military services.

DEDUCTIONS FROM WAGES

1. An employer may only make deductions from the wage of an employee for compensation for damage of tools and equipment of the employer.

2. An employee is entitled to know the reasons for his/her wage deductions.

3. Monthly deductions must not exceed 30% of the monthly wage of an employee after having paid compulsory social insurance, health insurance and unemployment insurance premiums and income tax.

BONUSES

1. Bonus is a sum of money paid by an employer to his/her employees on the basis of annual business results and the level of work performance of employees.

2. Bonus regulations must be decided and publicly announced by the employer at the workplace after consultation with the representative organization of the grassroots-level employees' collective.

NORMAL WORKING TIME

1. Normal working time must not exceed 8 hours per day or 48 hours per week.

2. An employer may determine the working time on an hourly, daily or weekly basis; in case of working on a weekly basis, the normal working time must not exceed 10 hours per day and not exceed 48 hours per week.

The State encourages employers to apply 40 working hours per week.

3. The working time must not exceed 6 hours per day for employees who perform extremely heavy, hazardous or dangerous jobs.

WORKING HOURS AT NIGHT

Working hours at night are counted from 22:00 pm on the previous day to 06:00 am on the next day.

OVERTIME WORK

Overtime is time worked in addition to normal working hours prescribed in the law, collective labor agreements or internal working regulations.

REST BREAKS DURING WORKING HOURS

1. An employee who works for 8 hours consecutively or 6 hours is entitled to a break of at least 30 minutes in the middle of working which must be counted in the working hours.

2. An employee who works at night is entitled to a break of at least 45 minutes in the middle of working which must be counted in the working hours.

3. Besides the breaks in the middle of working, the employer shall determine other short breaks and include them in the internal working regulations.

BREAKS BETWEEN SHIFTS

Employees who work in shifts are entitled to a break of at least 12 hours before moving to another shift.

WEEKLY BREAKS

1. Every week, an employee is entitled to a break of at least 24 consecutive hours. In case it is impossible for an employee to have a weekly break due to the cycle of work, the employer shall ensure the employee have at least 4 days off on average in a month.

2. An employer may determine and schedule weekly breaks either on Sunday or another fixed weekday and shall include them in the internal working regulations.

ANNUAL LEAVE

1. An employee who has been working for an employer for full 12 months is entitled a fully paid annual leave as stated in his/her labor contract as follows:

a/ Twelve working days for an employee working in normal conditions;

b/ Fourteen working days for an employee doing a heavy, hazardous or dangerous job; or an employee working in a place with harsh living conditions;

c/ Sixteen working days for an employee doing an extremely heavy, hazardous or dangerous job; an employee working in a place with extremely harsh living conditions.

2. An employer may decide on a timetable for annual leaves of employees after consulting employees and shall notify it in advance to them.

3. An employee may reach an agreement with the employer on taking annual leave in installments or combining annual leaves of maximum every three years.

4. When taking annual leave, if an employee travels by road, railway or waterway and the return trip takes more than 2 days, the travel days from the 3rd day onward will be added to the annual leave and this will be applied for only one annual leave in a year.

PERSONAL LEAVE, UNPAID LEAVE

1. An employee may take fully paid leave for personal reasons in the following cases:

a/ Marriage: 3 days;

b/ Marriage of his/her child: 1 day;

c/ Death of a blood parent or a parent of his/her spouse, his/her spouse or child: 3 days.

2. An employee may take 1 day off without pay and shall inform the employer when a paternal or maternal grandparent or blood sibling dies; his/her father or mother gets married; or a blood sibling gets married.

LABOR DISCIPLINE

Labor discipline means regulations on compliance with time requirements, technology and production and business administration as stipulated in the internal working regulations.

INTERNAL WORKING REGULATIONS

1. An employer employing 10 or more employees must have internal working regulations in writing.

2. The contents of internal working regulations must not be contrary to the labor law and other relevant laws. The internal working regulations contain the following principal contents:

a/ Working time and rest time;

b/ Order at workplace;

c/ Occupational safety and hygiene at workplace;

d/ Protection of assets and technological and business secrets and intellectual property of the employer;

e/ Employees' violations of labor discipline, forms of dealing with violations of labor discipline, and material responsibilities.

3. Before the issuance of the internal working regulations, an employer shall consult the representative organization of the grassroots-level employees' collective.

4. The internal working regulations must be notified to employees and their key contents must be displayed at necessary places in the workplace.

PRINCIPLES AND ORDER FOR HANDLING VIOLATIONS OF LABOR DISCIPLINE

1. The handling of a violation of labor discipline is provided as follows:

a/ The employer shall prove the fault of the employee;

b/ The representative organization of the grassroots-level employees' collective must participate in the handling;

c/ The employee must be present and may defend himself/herself or ask a lawyer or another person to defend him/her; if the employee is under 18 years old, his/her parent or at-law representative must participate in the handling;

d/ The handling of the violation of labor discipline must be recorded in the minutes.

2. It is prohibited to impose more than one form of discipline for a single violation of labor discipline.

3. For an employee who simultaneously commits more than one violation of labor discipline, it is only allowed to apply the highest form of discipline corresponding to the most serious violation.

4. Labor discipline may not be imposed for violations committed by an employee who is currently:

a/ Taking sickness or convalescence leave or a leave with the employer's consent;

b/ Kept in custody or temporary detention;

c/ Waiting for results of verification and conclusion of a competent agency for acts of violation;

d/ A female employee and pregnant or on maternity leave; rearing a child under 12 months of age.

FORMS OF HANDLING OF VIOLATIONS OF LABOR DISCIPLINE

1. Reprimand.

2. Prolongation of the wage rise period for no more than 6 months; removal from office.

3. Dismissal.

APPLICATION OF DISMISSAL AS A FORM OF DISCIPLINE

Dismissal may be applied by an employer as a form of discipline in the following cases:

1. An employee commits an act of theft, embezzlement, gambling, intentional infliction of injury, use of drugs inside the workplace, disclosure of technological or business secrets or infringement of intellectual property rights of the employer, or acts which cause serious damage or threaten to cause serious damage to the assets or interests of the employer;

2. An employee who has been subject to the disciplinary measure of prolonging the wage rise period commits recidivism when the disciplinary record has not yet been written off or an employee who has been subject to the disciplinary measure of removal from office commits recidivism;

Recidivism means that an employee re-commits the same violation for which he/she has been disciplined while his/her disciplinary record has not yet been written off.

3. An employee has been absent from work without permission for a total of 5 working days within 1 month or 20 days within 1 year without plausible reasons.

Plausible reasons include natural disaster, fire, illness of the employee or his/her next of kin with certification by a competent health establishment and other events defined in the internal working regulations.

PROHIBITED ACTS WHEN HANDLING VIOLATIONS OF LABOR DISCIPLINE

1. Infringing upon the body or dignity of the employee.

2. Applying a fine or wage reduction instead of a disciplinary measure.

3. Disciplining an employee who has committed a violation which is not defined in the internal working regulations.

WORK SUSPENSION

1. An employer may suspend an employee from working if the employer considers that the case of violation is complex and any continued performance of the work by the employee can cause difficulties to verification work. Work suspension may only be applied after the representative organization of the grassroots-level employees' collective has been consulted.

2. The period of work suspension must not exceed 15 days, or 90 days in special cases. During the period of work suspension, the employee is entitled to 50 per cent of the wage he/she receives prior to the suspension.

Upon the expiry of the period of work suspension, the employer must receive the employee back to his/her work.

3. In case the employee is disciplined, he/she is not required to reimburse the wage advanced to him/her.

4. In case the employee is not disciplined, the employer shall pay the full wage for the period of work suspension.

COMPENSATION FOR DAMAGE

1. An employee who causes damage to tools and equipment or the assets of the employer shall pay compensation in accordance with law.

2. An employee who loses tools, equipment or assets of the employer or other assets assigned to him/her by the employer, or uses supplies in excess of the permitted norms shall compensate the whole or a part of the damage at the market price; in case a contract of responsibility has been signed, the amount of compensation must comply with such contract; in case the damage is caused by a natural disaster, fire, enemy sabotage, epidemic, calamity or another objective event which is unforeseeable and irremediable and every necessary measure has been taken to full ability, no compensation is required.

LABOR ACCIDENTS

1. Labor accident is an accident that causes injury to any bodily part and function of an employee or causes death, and occurs during the performance of work and in connection with the performance of a job or task.

This provision also applies to apprentices, on-the-job trainees and employees on probation.

2. Victims of labor accidents must be promptly provided with first aid and adequate treatment.

3. All labor accidents, occupational diseases and serious incidents happening at workplace must be notified, investigated, documented, statistically calculated and reported on a regular basis according to the Government's regulations.

OCCUPATIONAL DISEASES

1. Occupational disease is an illness caused by the harmful working conditions of an occupation on an employee.

2. An employee suffering an occupational disease must be provided with adequate treatment and regular checks-up and have a separate medical record.

EMPLOYERS' RESPONSIBILITIES FOR LABOR ACCIDENTS AND OCCUPATIONAL DISEASES OF EMPLOYEES

1. To bear the part of the costs which must be jointly paid and costs which are not covered by health insurance for employees who have health insurance; to pay all medical expenses incurred from first aid and emergency aid until stable treatment for employees who do not have health insurance.

2. To pay full wages under labor contracts to employees who have labor accidents or suffer occupational diseases during the medical treatment period.

3. To pay compensations to employees who have labor accidents or suffer occupational diseases.

RIGHTS OF EMPLOYEES WHO HAVE LABOR ACCIDENTS OR SUFFER OCCUPATIONAL DISEASES

1. An employee who participates in compulsory social insurance is entitled to the benefit regime for labor accidents and occupational diseases as provided by the Law on Social Insurance.

2. For an employee subject to compulsory social insurance whose employer has not paid social insurance premiums to the social insurance agency, the employer shall pay an amount of money equal to the regime for labor accidents and occupational diseases as provided by the Law on Social Insurance.

The payment may be paid in a lump sum or on a monthly basis as agreed upon by the parties.

PROHIBITED ACTS IN OCCUPATIONAL SAFETY AND HYGIENE

1. Making cash payments instead of providing in-kind allowances to employees.

2. Concealing or falsely declaring or reporting on labor accidents and occupational diseases.

OCCUPATIONAL SAFETY AND HYGIENE PLANS

Annually, when developing business and production plans, employers shall prepare plans and measures for occupational safety and hygiene and improvement of working conditions.

PERSONAL PROTECTION EQUIPMENT IN WORK

1. An employee doing a dangerous or toxic job must be adequately provided with and shall use personal protection equipment in the working process.

2. Personal protection equipment must meet applicable quality standards.

INFORMATION ON OCCUPATIONAL SAFETY AND HYGIENE

Employers shall provide adequate information on the situation of labor accidents, occupational diseases and dangerous and harmful factors and measures to ensure occupational safety and hygiene for employees at workplace.

HEALTH CARE FOR EMPLOYEES

1. Based on health criteria for each type of work, an employer shall recruit and arrange work for employees.

2. Annually, an employer shall organize periodical health checks-up for employees, including apprentices and on-the-job trainees, obstetrics and gynecology checks for female employees, and health checks-up at least once every 6 months for employees doing heavy and harmful jobs and disabled, minor and elderly employees.

3. An employee who works in conditions with risks of occupational disease must have occupational disease checks.

4. An employee who has a labor accident or suffers an occupational disease shall undergo a medical assessment to determine his/her level of injury or disability and the level of working ability loss, and is entitled to treatment, care and working ability rehabilitation in accordance with law.

STATE POLICIES TOWARD FEMALE EMPLOYEES

1. To protect the female employees' right to employment equality.

2. To encourage employers to create conditions for female employees to have regular employment, and to extensively implement systems of flexible working hours, part-time work or home-based work for female employees.

3. To introduce measures to create employment opportunities, improve working conditions, raise vocational qualifications and healthcare, and increase material and spiritual welfare for female employees in order to assist them in effectively bringing into play their vocational capacity and harmoniously combining their working lives with family lives.

4. To formulate policies on tax reductions for employers using many female employees in accordance with tax laws.

5. To develop various forms of training which are favorable for female employees to acquire standby vocational skills suitable to their physical and physiological characteristics and their motherhood function.

OBLIGATIONS OF EMPLOYERS TOWARD FEMALE EMPLOYEES

1. To ensure gender equality and implement measures to promote gender equality in recruitment, employment, training, working time, rest time, wages and other policies.

2. To consult female employees or their representatives when taking decisions on issues related to the rights and interests of women.

3. To ensure sufficient bathrooms and appropriate toilets in the workplace.

4. To assist and support in building crèches and kindergartens, or cover part of childcare expenses at crèches and kindergartens incurred by female employees.

PROTECTION OF MATERNITY FOR FEMALE EMPLOYEES

1. An employer may not mobilize female employees to work at night, work overtime or go on a long working trip in the following cases:

a/ The employee is in her seventh month of pregnancy, or in her sixth month of pregnancy in case of working in a mountainous, remote, distant, border or island area;

b/ The employee is nursing a child under 12 months of age.

2. A female employee who performs heavy work, upon reaching her seventh month of pregnancy, is entitled to be transferred to a lighter work or have her daily working time reduced by 1 hour while still receiving her full wage.

3. An employer may neither dismiss a female employee nor unilaterally terminate the labor contract with a female employee for the reason of her marriage, pregnancy, maternity leave, or that she is nursing a child under 12 months of age, except the case in which the employer is an individual who dies, or is declared by a court to have lost his/her civil act capacity, or to be missing or dead, or the employer is an institution that ceases operation.

4. Labor disciplinary measures may not applied to a female employee during the time of pregnancy or maternity leave as provided by the law on social insurance, or nursing a child under 12 months of age.

5. A female employee in her menstruation period is entitled to a 30-minute break in every working day; a female employee nursing a child under 12 months of age is entitled to a 60-minute break in every working day with full wage as stated in the labor contract.

RIGHT OF PREGNANT EMPLOYEES TO UNILATERALLY TERMINATE OR POSTPONE LABOR CONTRACTS

In case a pregnant employee has a certificate of a competent health establishment which states that continued work will adversely affect her pregnancy, she may unilaterally terminate the labor contract or temporarily postpone the performance of the labor contract. The period for the female employee to give advance notice to the employer depends on the period determined by the competent health establishment.

MATERNITY LEAVE

1. A female employee is entitled to 6 months of prenatal and postnatal leave.

In case a female employee gives birth to twin or more babies, counting from the second child upward, for each child the mother is entitled to 1 more month off.

Prenatal leave must not exceed 2 months.

2. During the maternity leave, a female employee is entitled to maternity policies provided by the law on social insurance.

3. After the maternity leave period, if a female employee wishes, she may take additional leave without pay as agreed upon with the employer.

ALLOWANCES FOR LEAVE FOR CARING A SICK CHILD, FOR PREGNANCY CHECKS-UP AND FOR APPLYING CONTRACEPTIVE MEASURES

When taking leaves for pregnancy check-up, miscarriage, abortion, dead or diseased fetus in womb, for applying contraceptive measures, caring a sick child who is under 7 years of age or for nursing an adopted child under 6 months of age, a female employee is entitled to social insurance allowance in accordance with the law on social insurance.

PROHIBITED WORK FOR FEMALE EMPLOYEES

1. Work that is harmful to child bearing and nursing functions.

2. Work that requires the body constantly immersed in water.

3. Regular underground work in mines.

MINOR EMPLOYEES

A minor employee is an employee under 18 years of age.

EMPLOYMENT OF MINORS

1. An employer may only employ minors in work suitable to their health so as to ensure their physical, spiritual and personality development, and shall take care of minor employees regarding their work, wage, health and training in the course of their employment.

2. When employing minors, an employer shall keep a separate register fully recorded with the name, date of birth, work assigned, results of periodical medical checks of each minor employee, and shall present it at the request of a competent state agency.

PRINCIPLES OF EMPLOYMENT OF MINORS

1. Employment of minors is prohibited in heavy, toxic and dangerous jobs or in workplaces or jobs which may adversely affect their personality.

2. The working time of minor employees aged from full 15 years to under 18 years must not exceed 8 hours per day and 40 hours per week.

The working time of employees aged under 15 years must not exceed 4 hours per day and 20 hours per week and the employer may not employ these minors to work overtime or at night.

3. An employer may not employ minors to manufacture and trade in alcohol, wine, beer, cigarettes, stimulants and other habit-forming substances.

4. An employer shall create opportunities for minor employees and employed persons aged under 15 years to receive general education.

PROHIBITED JOBS AND WORKPLACES FOR MINOR EMPLOYEES

1. Employment of minors is prohibited in the following jobs:

a/ Carrying and lifting of heavy objects which are beyond a minor's physical strength;

b/ Manufacture, use or transportation of chemicals, gas and explosives;

c/ Maintenance of equipment and machines;

d/ Demolition of construction works;

e/ Melting, blowing, casting, rolling, molding and welding of metals;

f/ Sea diving, offshore fishing;

g/ Other jobs which are harmful to the health, safety or morality of minor employees.

2. Employment of minors is prohibited in the following workplaces:

a/ Underwater, underground, in cave and in tunnel;

b/ Construction site;

c/ Slaughter house;

d/ Casino, bar, dance hall, karaoke parlor, hotel, hostel, sauna, massage room;

e/ Other workplaces which are harmful to the health, safety or morality of minor employees.

ELDERLY EMPLOYEES

1. Elderly employees are entitled to reduced daily working hours or to the regime of part-time work.

2. In the last working year before retirement, elderly employees are entitled to reduced normal working hours or to the regime of part-time work.

EMPLOYMENT OF ELDERLY EMPLOYEES

1. If, after retirement, an elderly employee is employed under a new labor contract, he/she still enjoys the rights and interests agreed upon in the labor contract, in addition to the rights and benefits under the retirement regime.

2. An employer may not employ elderly employees in heavy or dangerous jobs or jobs exposed to toxic substances that adversely affect their health, except in special cases as stipulated by the Government.

3. An employer is responsible for taking care of the health of elderly employees at the workplace.

EMPLOYMENT OF DISABLED PERSONS

1. An employer shall ensure working conditions, working tools and occupational safety and hygiene suitable to disabled employees and take regular care for their health.

2. An employer shall consult disabled employees before deciding on matters involving their rights and interests.

PROHIBITED ACTS IN EMPLOYMENT OF DISABLED PERSONS

1. Employing a disabled person who has lost 51% or more of his/her working ability to work overtime and at night.

2. Employing a disabled person to perform a heavy or dangerous job or a job exposed to toxic substances.

Conclusion

Thank you again for downloading this book on *"LABOR LAW: Essential Legal Terms Explained You Need To Know About Law On Labor"* and reading all the way to the end. I'm extremely grateful.

If you know of anyone else who may benefit from the informative legal words presented in this book, please help me inform them of this book. I would greatly appreciate it.

Finally, if you enjoyed this book and feel that it has added value to your study or career in any way, please take a couple of minutes to share your thoughts and post a REVIEW on Amazon. Your feedback will help me to continue to write the kind of Kindle books that helps you get results. Furthermore, if you write a simple REVIEW with positive words for this book on Amazon, you can help hundreds or perhaps thousands of other readers who may want to enhance their legal vocabulary have a chance getting what they need. Like you, they worked hard for every penny they spend on books. With the information and recommendation you provide, they would be more likely to take action right away. We really look forward to reading your review.

Thanks again for your support and good luck!

If you enjoy my book, please write a POSITIVE REVIEW on amazon.

-- Dr. Peter Johnson --

Check Out Other Books

Go here to check out other related books that might interest you:

Legal Terminology And Phrases: Essential Legal Terms Explained You Need To Know About Crimes, Penalty And Criminal Procedure

http://www.amazon.com/dp/B01L5EB54Y

COMPANY LAW: Mastering Essential Legal Terms Explained About Limited Liability Companies, Joint-Stock Companies, Partnership, Private Enterprises, And Groups of Companies!

https://www.amazon.com/dp/B07P2PRVMJ

INVESTMENT LAW: Essential Legal Terms Explained You Need To Know About Law On Investment!

https://www.amazon.com/dp/B07P79D925

CIVIL LAW: Mastering Essential Legal Terms Explained About Civil Rights, Guardianship, Civil Transactions, Civil Obligations, Civil Liability, Civil Contracts And Civil Procedure!

https://www.amazon.com/dp/B07P5GS8LD

Legal Vocabulary In Use: Master 600+ Essential Legal Terms And Phrases Explained In 10 Minutes A Day

http://www.amazon.com/dp/B01L0FKXPU

Civil Law Vocabulary In Use: Master 350+ Essential Civil Law Terms And Phrases Explained With Examples In 10 Minutes A Day.

https://www.amazon.com/dp/B0781TQWGV

Criminal Law Vocabulary In Use: Master 400+ Essential Criminal Law Terms And Phrases Explained With Examples In 10 Minutes A Day.

https://www.amazon.com/dp/B078KLR51Z

Administrative And Tax Law In Use : Master 300+ Administrative And Tax Law Terms And Phrases Explained With Examples In 10 Minutes A Day.

https://www.amazon.com/dp/B07JMD546J

Productivity Secrets For Students: The Ultimate Guide To Improve Your Mental Concentration, Kill Procrastination, Boost Memory And Maximize Productivity In Study

http://www.amazon.com/dp/B01JS52UT6

Shortcut To Ielts Writing: The Ultimate Guide To Immediately Increase Your Ielts Writing Scores

http://www.amazon.com/dp/B01JV7EQGG

www.ingramcontent.com/pod-product-compliance
Lightning Source LLC
Chambersburg PA
CBHW030714220526
45463CB00005B/2037